CASSEROLES AND STEWS

Norma MacMillan

GOLDEN PRESS / NEW YORK
Western Publishing Company, Inc.
Racine, Wisconsin

christmas '85

Mum & Dad

CONTENTS

NOTES:

Always preheat the oven to the specified temperature.

Margarine can be substituted for butter in all recipes.

This edition prepared under the supervision of Joanna Morris

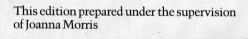

This edition published 1984 by Golden Press
Library of Congress Catalog Card Number: 84-80336
ISBN 0-307-09967-9
Golden® and Golden Press® are registered trademarks
of Western Publishing Company, Inc.

First published in 1979 in the U.K. by Cathay Books,
59 Grosvenor Street, London W1

© 1984, 1983, 1981, 1980, 1979 Cathay Books

Printed in Hong Kong

INTRODUCTION

What comes to mind when you see a casserole recipe in a cookbook? A piping hot, nourishing meal on a freezing winter day? A sophisticated dinner party main dish? A simple way of experimenting with new and exotic cuisines? The casserole is all these, and more.

All kinds of ingredients can make up a casserole – fish, meat, poultry, vegetables, beans, pasta, rice and cheese. And by its very nature, the casserole is simplicity itself.

Most casseroles require little attention during cooking – they can be popped into the oven and simply forgotten about for an hour or so. With the aid of a timer that can turn your oven on and off, you can return to a delicious cooked casserole after a hectic day. And yet, not all casseroles take hours to cook: Those prepared from leftovers and convenience foods can be ready in about half an hour.

Whether you are feeding a hungry family or giving a dinner party, you'll find that a casserole is the ideal answer – and this cookbook offers a wide range of choices.

BEEF

Braised Beef in Beer

2 tablespoons butter
2 tablespoons oil
2½ lb stewing beef,
    cut into cubes
3 onions, chopped
1 tablespoon brandy
2¼ cups beer
Bouquet garni
1 lb carrots, cut up
½ lb small turnips,
    halved
1 medium eggplant,
    cut into 1-inch
    cubes
6 mushrooms
Salt and pepper

Heat the butter and oil in a 4-quart Dutch oven, add the beef cubes and brown well.

Add the onions and sauté until soft. Add the brandy and ignite. When the flames have died down, add the beer, bouquet garni, carrots, turnips and eggplant.

Bring to a boil and simmer gently on top of the range; or cook in a 350° oven for about 3 hours, or until the beef is very tender. Add the mushrooms, and salt and pepper to taste, for the last 30 minutes. Discard the bouquet garni.
6 servings

Oxtail with Grapes

2 tablespoons butter
4 lb oxtail
1 lb onions, chopped
1 lb large carrots,
    halved lengthwise
1¼ cups boiling beef
    broth
1¼ cups white wine
½ lb seedless green
    grapes, crushed
Salt and pepper

Melt the butter in a 6-quart Dutch oven and sauté the oxtail until well browned; remove. Add the onions and sauté for 1 to 2 minutes. Return the oxtail to the pot and add the remaining ingredients. Cover and simmer over low heat for about 4 hours.

Arrange the oxtail on a large, warmed serving dish with the carrots down one side; keep hot. Skim the fat from the sauce and, if necessary, boil down to thicken. Serve with the sauce poured over the oxtail.

4 to 6 servings

Daube de Boeuf

1 large onion, sliced
2 large carrots, sliced
1¼ cups dry white wine
2 cloves garlic, crushed
1 bay leaf
1 teaspoon dried thyme
3 lb stewing beef, cut into cubes
¼ cup flour
Salt and pepper
6 slices bacon, diced
2 teaspoons grated orange rind
1 can (16 oz) whole tomatoes, drained and chopped
½ lb mushrooms, sliced
12 black olives
⅔ cup beef broth

Mix together the onion, carrots, wine, garlic, bay leaf and thyme in a large bowl. Add the beef cubes. Cover and marinate overnight in the refrigerator.

Drain the beef, reserving the marinade, and pat dry with paper towels. Season the flour with salt and pepper and use to coat the beef.

Put one-third of the bacon in a 4-quart Dutch oven. Spoon in half the marinade, then add half the beef. Sprinkle with half the orange rind, then add half the tomatoes and mushrooms.

Repeat the layers, then top with the olives and the remaining bacon. Pour in the broth.

Bring to a boil, cover and transfer to a 325° oven; bake for 4 hours, or until tender. Discard the bay leaf and check the seasoning. Serve with parsleyed boiled potatoes.
6 to 8 servings

Oxtail Casserole

¼ cup flour
Salt and pepper
4 lb oxtail
3 tablespoons brandy
2 onions, chopped
5 carrots, chopped
Bouquet garni
1½ cups dry red wine
2 cups beef broth or water

Season the flour with salt and pepper and use to coat the oxtail. Place in a 6-quart Dutch oven and roast in a 450° oven for 30 minutes, turning often.

Drain off all the fat from the pot. Warm the brandy, pour over the oxtail and ignite. When the flames have died down, add the onions, carrots, bouquet garni, wine and broth.

Reduce the oven to 350° and bake for 4 hours, or until the oxtail is tender. Stir during cooking and add liquid if necessary. Discard the bouquet garni. Serve with rice or cracked wheat.
4 to 6 servings

Lemon Beef Stew

1 tablespoon oil
2 lb stewing beef, cut
　into cubes
2 large onions,
　chopped
1 large lemon, peeled
　and chopped
1 green pepper,
　seeded and cut
　into rings
1 can (16 oz) crushed
　tomatoes
2 teaspoons
　Worcestershire
　sauce
Salt and pepper

Pour the oil into a shallow 3-quart baking dish and add the beef cubes and onions. Cook in a 450° oven for 30 minutes, or until the beef is browned on all sides, stirring frequently.

Reduce the heat to 350°. Cover the beef with the chopped lemon and green pepper rings. Mix together the tomatoes and their juice, Worcestershire, salt and pepper and pour on top. Cover and bake 1½ hours, or until the beef is tender. If necessary, add a little water or broth during cooking. Serve with mashed or boiled potatoes.

4 servings

Italian Beef Casserole

2 tablespoons oil
1 onion, chopped
1 clove garlic,
    chopped
4 slices bacon, diced
2 carrots, diced
1 stalk celery, diced
1 lb lean ground beef
1 can (10¾ oz)
    condensed tomato
    soup, undiluted
1 can (16 oz) whole
    tomatoes, drained
1 teaspoon dried
    basil
4 cups egg noodles
Salt and pepper
1 cup shredded
    Cheddar cheese

Heat the oil in a 10-inch skillet, add the onion, garlic and bacon and sauté until the onion is soft. Add the carrots and celery and continue cooking for 3 minutes. Stir in the beef and brown. Drain off any excess fat, then add the soup, tomatoes and basil. Simmer for about 15 minutes.

Meanwhile, cook the noodles in boiling salted water until just tender. Drain. Add the noodles to the beef mixture and fold together. Add salt and pepper to taste, then transfer to a 2-quart baking dish. Sprinkle the cheese on top. Cook in a 350° oven for 30 minutes. Serve with a crisp salad.

4 servings

Beef and Spinach Bake

1½ lb spinach
1 tablespoon oil
1 large onion, finely chopped
1 lb lean ground beef
½ lb mushrooms, sliced
¾ cup sour cream
½ teaspoon each dried marjoram, thyme and basil
1 cup shredded Cheddar cheese
1 cup grated Parmesan cheese
Salt and pepper

Cook the spinach, with only the water clinging to the leaves after washing, until just wilted. Drain well, pressing out all the excess water with paper towels, and chop.

Heat the oil in a 10-inch skillet. Add the onion and sauté until soft. Add the beef and brown. Stir in the mushrooms and cook 5 minutes longer. Remove from the heat and drain off all the fat from the skillet. Add the chopped spinach, sour cream, herbs, half of the Cheddar and half of the Parmesan cheese. Mix well, adding salt and pepper to taste, then pour into a 12 × 7½-inch baking dish.

Sprinkle the remaining cheeses on top. Bake in a 350° oven for 25 minutes. Serve with rice and a green salad.
4 servings

NOTE: For variety, sauté the onion with 1 clove of garlic, chopped.

Chili-Pasta Casserole

This is a particularly good version of chili, one that can be on the table within an hour. As with all chili recipes, let your personal taste be the guide when adding chili powder.

2 tablespoons oil
1 medium onion, chopped
1 lb lean ground beef
1 can (16 oz) whole tomatoes
2 tablespoons tomato paste
1 green pepper, seeded and diced
1 tablespoon chili powder
½ lb small pasta shells
1 can (16 oz) red kidney beans, drained
1 cup shredded sharp Cheddar cheese

Heat the oil in a 10-inch skillet, add the onion and sauté until soft. Add the beef and brown well. Drain off excess fat, then stir in the tomatoes with their juice, tomato paste, green pepper and chili powder. Simmer for 15 minutes.

Meanwhile, cook the pasta shells in boiling salted water until just tender. Drain.

Mix the kidney beans into the chili mixture, then fold in the pasta shells. Add salt and pepper to taste. Transfer to a 2½-quart casserole and sprinkle the cheese on top. Bake in a 350° oven for 30 minutes. Serve with a green salad.

4 servings

Ginger Beef

¼ cup flour
1 teaspoon ground ginger
Salt and pepper
2 lb stewing beef, cut into cubes
¼ cup oil
1 large onion, chopped
1 clove garlic, chopped
1 can (16 oz) crushed tomatoes
2 tablespoons tomato paste
1¼ cups beef broth
2 tablespoons soy sauce

Season the flour with ginger and a little salt and pepper and use to coat the beef cubes.

Heat the oil in a 10-inch skillet. Add the beef and brown on all sides. Transfer to a 4-quart Dutch oven.

Add the onion and garlic to the skillet and sauté until soft. Stir in the tomatoes, tomato paste, beef broth, soy sauce and salt and pepper to taste. Pour into the pot, cover and bake in a 350° oven for 2½ to 3 hours, or until the beef is tender. Garnish with chopped parsley. Serve with rice or cracked wheat and a green salad.

4 to 6 servings

Illustrated above:
Ginger Beef;
Pot Roast with
Horseradish (page 14)

Pot Roast with Horseradish

1/4 cup flour
Salt and pepper
1 chuck or rump
    roast (2 1/2 lb)
2 tablespoons oil
6 tablespoons
    prepared
    horseradish
1 cup beef broth or
    water
6 potatoes, halved
6 carrots, sliced
12 small white
    onions

Season the flour with salt and pepper and use to coat the beef. Heat the oil in a 4-quart Dutch oven, add the beef and brown. Spread the horseradish over the beef and pour in the broth. Cover tightly and bake in a 325° oven for 2 1/2 hours.

Add the vegetables and salt and pepper to taste. Cover the pot and bake 1 hour longer, or until the meat and vegetables are tender.

4 servings

Illustrated on page 13

Beef Stroganoff Casserole

2 tablespoons butter
2 lb rump, round or
    chuck steak, cut
    into 1/4-inch-thick
    strips
1 tablespoon oil
1 onion, sliced
1/2 lb mushrooms,
    sliced
2 tablespoons flour
3/4 cup beef broth
1 1/2 tablespoons
    tomato paste
Salt and pepper
3/4 cup sour cream

Melt the butter in a 10-inch skillet, add the beef strips and brown evenly on both sides. Transfer the beef to a 1 1/2-quart casserole.

Add the oil to the skillet and heat, then add the onion and mushrooms and sauté until the onion is soft. Sprinkle in the flour and cook, stirring, for 2 minutes. Gradually stir in the broth. Remove from the heat and add the tomato paste, salt and pepper. Pour the onion mixture over the beef and stir.

Cover tightly and bake in a 325° oven for 1 hour, or until the beef is tender. Stir in the sour cream and garnish with chopped parsley. Heat through. Serve with rice and buttered spinach.

4 servings

Beef Carbonnade

4 tablespoons oil
2 lb stewing beef, cut
  into cubes
2 onions, sliced
2 tablespoons flour
1 can (12 oz) beer
1½ cups beef broth
Bouquet garni
Pinch of grated
  nutmeg
Pinch of sugar
1½ teaspoons wine
  vinegar
Salt and pepper

Heat the oil in a 3-quart Dutch oven. Add the beef cubes, a few at a time, and brown on all sides. Remove the beef and set aside.

Add the onions to the pot; sauté until golden brown. Sprinkle in the flour and cook, stirring, for 2 minutes. Gradually stir in the beer and broth and bring to a boil. Add the bouquet garni, nutmeg, sugar, vinegar, salt and pepper. Return the beef to the pot and stir.

Cover tightly and bake in a 325° oven for 2 hours, or until the beef is tender. Discard the bouquet garni and serve with a green vegetable and boiled potatoes.
4 servings

Beef Stew with Dumplings

The secret of good dumplings is to steam them on top of the stew, not in it.

1 tablespoon oil
1½ lb stewing beef, cut into cubes
1½ cups beef broth
1 tablespoon tomato paste
Salt and pepper
2 onions, quartered
2 stalks celery, thickly sliced
4 carrots, sliced
2 turnips, diced
1 cup all-purpose flour
2 teaspoons baking powder
¾ teaspoon salt
¼ cup shortening
¾ cup milk

Heat the oil in a 2-quart flameproof casserole, add the beef cubes and brown, adding additional oil if necessary. Add the broth, tomato paste, salt and pepper. Cover and bring to a boil. Simmer on top of the range or bake in a 350° oven for 1½ hours.

Add the vegetables and continue cooking for 1 hour, or until the beef and vegetables are tender.

Place the flour, baking powder and salt in a bowl. Cut in the shortening until the dough resembles bread crumbs. Stir in the milk. Drop the batter by the spoonful on top of the stew; cook uncovered for 10 minutes.

Cover and steam for 10 minutes. Serve with a crisp green salad and fresh fruit for dessert.

4 servings

Scandinavian Meatballs

1 lb ground beef
Grated nutmeg
Salt and pepper
1 egg
½ cup dry bread
   crumbs
2 tablespoons oil
¼ lb gherkins, sliced
   lengthwise
1 clove garlic,
   chopped
1 cup egg noodles
1 cauliflower,
   broken into
   flowerets
1¼ cups chicken
   broth
⅔ cup sour cream
1 teaspoon chopped
   dill
8 pickled beets,
   diced
1 tablespoon vinegar

Put the beef in a bowl and season with nutmeg, salt and pepper. Add the egg and bread crumbs and mix lightly. Form into about 20 balls.

Heat the oil in a 10-inch skillet, add the meatballs and sauté until lightly browned, shaking the skillet occasionally to prevent them from sticking. Add the gherkins, garlic, noodles, cauliflower, broth, salt and pepper. Bring to a boil, cover and simmer for 25 minutes.

Transfer to a warmed serving dish. Pour the sour cream into a circle on top and sprinkle with the dill. Toss the beets in the vinegar, drain and pile in the center.
4 servings

Swiss Steak

3 tablespoons oil
3 large onions, sliced
2 stalks celery, sliced
1 rump or chuck steak (1½ lb), cut into 4 pieces
Salt and pepper
2 tablespoons flour
1 can (16 oz) crushed tomatoes
1 tablespoon tomato paste
1 clove garlic, chopped

Heat the oil in a 10-inch skillet and add the onions and celery; sauté gently until just colored. Transfer to a 2-quart baking dish.

Sprinkle the steaks with salt and pepper and coat with flour. Add to the skillet and brown both sides, then place in the baking dish.

Sprinkle any leftover flour into the skillet and blend into the fat; cook, stirring, for 1 minute, then add the remaining ingredients. Bring to the boil and pour over the steaks.

Cover and bake in a 325° oven for 1½ to 2 hours, or until the steaks are tender. Garnish with chopped parsley and serve with boiled potatoes and a green vegetable.

4 servings

Chili con Carne

1 lb lean ground beef
1 large onion, chopped
½ green pepper, chopped
1 can (14½ oz) whole tomatoes
2 tablespoons tomato paste
1 clove garlic, chopped
1 tablespoon chili powder
¼ teaspoon cayenne pepper
1 can (15½ oz) red kidney beans
Salt and pepper
1 tablespoon cornstarch blended with 2 tablespoons water

Put the beef in a 10-inch skillet and brown. Add the onion and green pepper and cook until soft.

Stir in the tomatoes with their juice, tomato paste, garlic, chili powder and cayenne. Bring to the boil, cover and simmer for about 50 minutes, stirring occasionally.

Stir in the kidney beans and salt and pepper to taste. Bring to the boil, cover and simmer for 20 minutes, stirring occasionally. Stir in the cornstarch and simmer, stirring, for 2 to 3 minutes. Serve with rice and a salad.

4 servings

PORK

Pork Chops with Plum Sauce

1 tablespoon butter
1 tablespoon oil
4 center cut pork
   chops, 1 inch
   thick
¼ cup water
1 lb purple plums,
   pitted
Sugar
½ teaspoon ground
   allspice
¾ cup dry red wine
Salt and pepper

Melt the butter with the oil in a 10-inch skillet. Add the chops and brown on both sides, then transfer to a shallow 2-quart casserole.

Add the water to the skillet and bring to a boil, scraping the skillet; add the plums, sugar to taste and allspice. Simmer until the plums are very soft. Allow to cool slightly, then puree in a blender. Mix in the red wine, salt and pepper. Pour over the chops. Add enough wine to just cover the chops.

Cover and bake in a 350° oven for 45 minutes, or until the chops are tender. Garnish with watercress and serve with carrots and scalloped potatoes (see page 77).

4 servings

Pork Chops with Plum Sauce;
Pork and Green Beans;
Pork in Mushroom
Sauce (page 22)

Pork and Green Beans

3 tablespoons flour
½ teaspoon ground
  ginger
Salt and pepper
2 lb lean pork, cut
  into 1-inch cubes
2 tablespoons butter
2 tablespoons oil
2 onions, thinly
  sliced
1 clove garlic,
  crushed
2 cups chicken broth
1 can (8 oz) tomato
  sauce
¾ lb green beans,
  trimmed and cut
  into 2-inch
  lengths

Season the flour with the ginger and a little salt and pepper and use to coat the pork cubes. Melt the butter with the oil in a 4-quart Dutch oven. Add the onions and garlic and sauté until softened. Add the pork and brown on all sides. Stir in enough broth to cover the pork and bring to a boil. Cover the pot and bake in a 325° oven for 2½ hours.

Skim any fat from the surface, then stir in the tomato sauce. Place the beans on top and press down gently so they become moistened with the cooking liquid. Cover the pot and bake 30 minutes longer. Serve with crusty bread.

4 servings

Pork in Mushroom Sauce

4 tablespoons butter
2 tablespoons oil
2 lb pork tenderloin,
  sliced
1 large onion, sliced
1 ¼ cups dry red
  wine
Salt and pepper
½ lb mushrooms,
  sliced
2 tablespoons flour
1 cup heavy cream

Melt the butter with the oil in a 10-inch skillet. Add the pork and brown on both sides. Remove from the skillet to a flameproof 3-quart casserole.

Add the onion to the skillet and sauté until soft. Drain and arrange over the pork. Add the wine and season with salt and pepper.

Cover and bake in a 350° oven for 1 ¼ hours. Stir in the mushrooms and continue baking for 15 minutes, or until the pork is tender.

Mix the flour and cream; stir into the casserole. Cook gently on top of the range, stirring, until the liquid has thickened; do not boil. Garnish with chives and serve with mashed potatoes and a green vegetable.

4 servings

Illustrated on page 21

Spicy Pork Ribs

8 country-style pork
  ribs
Salt and pepper
2 tablespoons butter
1 tablespoon oil
1 onion, chopped
1 clove garlic,
  crushed
1 cup catsup
2 cups water
¼ cup cider vinegar
¼ cup
  Worcestershire
  sauce
¼ cup brown sugar
1 teaspoon chili
  powder
Few drops of hot
  pepper sauce
8 lemon slices

Rub the ribs with salt and pepper on both sides. Melt the butter with the oil in a 10-inch skillet. Add the ribs, a few at a time, and brown on both sides; transfer them to a baking dish, arranging them in a single layer if possible.

Add the onion and garlic to the skillet and sauté until soft. Stir in the catsup, water, vinegar, Worcestershire, brown sugar, chili powder and hot pepper sauce; bring to a boil. Simmer for 30 minutes.

Taste the sauce and adjust seasoning. Place a lemon slice on each rib, then pour the sauce over them. Bake in a 350° oven for 1 ½ hours, or until the ribs are tender, turning occasionally. Serve with baked sweet potatoes and a spinach salad.

4 servings

Chili Pork

2 tablespoons oil
1 large onion,
    chopped
1 green pepper,
    seeded and diced
2 lb lean pork, cut
    into 1-inch cubes
1 can (10¾ oz)
    condensed tomato
    soup, undiluted
2 stalks celery,
    chopped
1 tablespoon chili
    powder
1 can (14½ oz) whole
    tomatoes, drained
    and chopped
1 can (16 oz) red
    kidney beans,
    drained
Salt and pepper

Heat the oil in a 4-quart Dutch oven. Add the onion and green pepper and sauté until soft. Stir in the pork cubes and brown lightly on all sides. Cover tightly and bake in a 350° oven for 40 minutes.

Stir in the soup, celery, chili powder and tomatoes. Cover and bake 20 minutes, or until the pork is tender.

Stir in the kidney beans; add salt and pepper to taste. Return to the oven, uncovered, for 10 minutes, or until the kidney beans are heated through. Serve with rice and tortillas or corn sticks.

4 servings

Alsatian Choucroute

1 tablespoon oil
4 slices bacon
4 pork chops,
 trimmed
1 can (10¼ oz)
 sauerkraut
½ lb carrots, halved
 lengthwise then
 crosswise
1 onion, sliced
6 juniper berries,
 lightly crushed
6 peppercorns
Salt
⅔ cup dry white
 wine
8 small potatoes
4 frankfurters

Heat the oil in a 4-quart Dutch oven, add the bacon and pork chops and brown lightly. Remove the chops.

Cover the bacon with half the sauerkraut, lay the chops on top and cover with the carrots and onion. Spread the remaining sauerkraut over the top and sprinkle with the juniper berries and peppercorns. Season lightly with salt and pour in the wine.

Bring to the boil, cover and simmer gently on top of the range or bake in a 325° oven for 45 minutes.

Add the potatoes, pushing them down into the sauerkraut. Score the frankfurters in a cross pattern and put on top. Cover and cook for 1 hour.

4 servings

New Orleans Jambalaya

2 tablespoons oil
8 chicken thighs
12 mini pork
 sausages
1 onion, chopped
2 cloves garlic,
 chopped
1 cup long-grain rice
1 can (16 oz) whole
 tomatoes
²⁄₃ cup dry white
 wine
1 teaspoon ground
 coriander
¼ teaspoon hot
 pepper sauce
1 teaspoon salt
1 green pepper,
 seeded and cut
 into rings
¼ to ½ lb cooked
 shrimp in shells

Heat the oil in a 4-quart Dutch oven; add the chicken and sausages and brown lightly; remove from the pot. Add the onion and garlic and sauté for 1 or 2 minutes. Stir in the rice. Add the tomatoes with their juice, wine, coriander, pepper sauce and salt. Return the chicken and sausages to the pot. Bring to a boil, cover and simmer for 20 minutes, or until the chicken is tender and the rice is done. Remove from the heat and stir.

Place the pepper rings and shrimp on top. Cover and leave for about 5 minutes. Serve with a green salad.

4 servings

Ham and Egg Casserole

4 medium potatoes
Salt and pepper
1 cup chopped
　cooked ham
6 hard-cooked eggs,
　sliced
1 cup shredded
　Cheddar cheese
4 green onions,
　thinly sliced
1 cup sour cream
2 tomatoes, sliced

Cook the potatoes in boiling salted water until tender. Drain, peel and slice.

Make alternate layers of potato, ham, eggs and cheese in a greased 2-quart casserole, sprinkling each layer of sliced eggs with salt, pepper and green onion. Begin and end with potatoes. Spread the sour cream over the top and arrange the sliced tomatoes in a ring. Bake in a 350° oven for 30 minutes. If desired, garnish with chopped chives

4 servings

Frank and Bean Casserole

1 lb frankfurters
2 tablespoons butter
1 large onion,
    chopped
2 cans (16 oz each)
    baked beans
½ cup finely
    chopped dried
    apricots
2 tablespoons brown
    sugar
1 teaspoon dry
    mustard

Slip the frankfurters into a pan of boiling water, remove from the heat and leave for 5 minutes. Drain the frankfurters and cut each into 4 pieces.

Melt the butter in a small skillet, add the onion and sauté until soft. Drain and put into a 3-quart casserole. Add the frankfurter pieces, baked beans, apricots, sugar and mustard. Cover and bake in a 350° oven for 30 to 45 minutes, or until heated through. Serve with a vegetable salad.

4 to 6 servings

Sausages with Cornbread

3 slices bacon
1 lb pork sausage
    links
2 onions, sliced
1 large carrot, diced
1 green pepper,
    seeded and diced
3 tablespoons flour
1½ cups cider
1 tablespoon
    Worcestershire
    sauce
Salt and pepper
TOPPING:
½ cup yellow
    cornmeal
½ cup flour
2 teaspoons baking
    powder
Pinch of sugar
¼ teaspoon salt
1 large egg
2 tablespoons butter,
    melted
½ cup milk

Sauté the bacon in a 10-inch skillet until crisp. Drain on paper towels and crumble.

Brown the sausages in the skillet. Remove from the skillet and cut in half. Pour off most of the fat from the pan.

Sauté the onions, carrot and green pepper for 2 or 3 minutes. Sprinkle in the flour and cook, stirring, 2 minutes. Gradually stir in the cider and bring to a boil, stirring; then stir in the Worcestershire, salt and pepper. Return the bacon and sausage to the skillet and stir. Cover and simmer while making the topping.

Mix together the cornmeal, flour, baking powder, sugar and salt. Beat in the egg, butter and enough milk to make a smooth thick batter.

Pour the sausage mixture into a deep baking dish not more than 8 inches in diameter. Pour the topping over the sausage mixture. Bake in a 425° oven for 15 to 20 minutes. Serve with a tossed salad.

4 servings.

Pork and Apple Casserole

2 tablespoons butter
2 large tart apples, peeled and sliced
1 large onion, chopped
2 teaspoons sugar
2 teaspoons dried sage
4 thick shoulder pork chops
Salt and pepper
1 cup sliced mushrooms
⅔ cup cider
1 cup soft bread crumbs
½ cup shredded sharp Cheddar cheese

Grease a shallow 3-quart baking dish with half the butter. Place half the apple slices in the baking dish and sprinkle with half the onion, sugar and sage. Arrange the pork chops on top, season with salt and pepper and cover with the mushrooms. Add the remaining apples, onion, sugar and sage. Pour in the cider.

Combine the bread crumbs and cheese and sprinkle over the top. Dot with the remaining butter. Bake in a 400° oven for 50 minutes, or until the chops are tender and the top is browned. Serve with baked potatoes.

4 servings

Pork and Fruit Casserole

1 tablespoon butter
1 tablespoon oil
4 center cut pork
   chops, 1 inch
   thick
1 can (16 oz) apricot
   halves
1 can (8¼ oz) sliced
   pineapple
8 prunes, pitted and
   chopped
2 tablespoons brown
   sugar
⅓ cup chicken broth
⅔ cup half-and-half
Salt and pepper

Melt the butter with the oil in a 10-inch skillet. Add the pork chops and brown on both sides. Remove the chops from the skillet, drain and arrange in a 2-quart baking dish.

Drain the apricot halves and sliced pineapple, reserving the syrups. Arrange the fruit over the chops. Add the prunes and sprinkle with the brown sugar.

Mix the broth with 5 tablespoons each of the apricot and pineapple syrups. Pour into the baking dish.

Cover with foil and bake in a 350° oven for about 1 hour, or until the chops are tender.

Transfer the chops to a warmed serving dish, being careful not to dislodge the fruit. Keep hot.

Pour the liquid into a saucepan and boil until reduced to about ⅔ cup. Skim off any fat, then stir in the half-and-half, salt and pepper. Heat through gently and pour into a warmed sauce dish. Serve with buttered noodles.

4 servings

LAMB

Irish Stew

4 tablespoons butter
2 lb boneless stewing
  lamb, cut into
  cubes
1 large onion,
  chopped
1 tablespoon flour
2 cups beef broth
Bouquet garni
4 potatoes, quartered
Salt and pepper

Melt the butter in a 4-quart Dutch oven. Add the lamb cubes and brown evenly, then remove and set aside. Add the onion and sauté until softened. Sprinkle with flour and stir. Return the lamb to the pot.

Pour in the beef broth and add the bouquet garni. Bring to a boil, cover and bake in a 350° oven for 1 hour.

Stir in the potatoes and salt and pepper to taste. Cover and bake for 45 minutes, or until the lamb and potatoes are tender. Remove the bouquet garni. If desired, garnish with chopped parsley and serve with a tossed salad.

4 servings

Irish Stew; Kidney Ragout;
Lamb Ratatouille (page 32)

Kidney Ragout

3 tablespoons flour
Salt and pepper
12 lamb kidneys or
   2 lb beef kidneys,
   sliced
½ lb sliced bacon
2 tablespoons butter
1 large onion, finely
   chopped
1 clove garlic,
   chopped
1 sweet red pepper,
   seeded and diced
1 can (8 oz) tomato
   sauce
⅔ cup beef broth
6 tablespoons red
   wine

Season the flour with salt and pepper and use to coat the kidney slices. Cook the bacon in a 10-inch skillet until crisp. Drain on paper towels, crumble and place in a 3-quart casserole. Drain all but 2 tablespoons of fat from the skillet.

Melt the butter in the skillet, add the kidney slices and brown quickly on both sides. Transfer to the casserole. Add the onion, garlic and red pepper to the skillet and sauté until the onion is soft. Stir in the tomato sauce, broth and wine and bring to a boil. Pour into the casserole and mix. Cover and bake in a 350° oven for 30 minutes, or until the kidneys are tender. Garnish with toast triangles and serve with diced potatoes and buttered zucchini.
4 servings

Lamb Ratatouille

1 large eggplant,
  halved lengthwise
  and sliced
Salt and pepper
¼ cup olive oil
2 lb boneless stewing
  lamb, cut into
  cubes
1 large onion, sliced
1½ lb zucchini,
  sliced
½ sweet red and
  ½ green pepper,
  seeded and sliced
1 can (16 oz) whole
  tomatoes
1 teaspoon dried
  basil

Sprinkle the eggplant slices with salt and let stand for 30 minutes. Rinse and pat dry.

Heat 3 tablespoons of the oil in a 4-quart Dutch oven. Add the lamb cubes and brown on all sides; remove and set aside.

Add the onion to the pot, with the remaining oil if necessary, and sauté until softened. Add the eggplant, zucchini, peppers, tomatoes with their juice, basil, salt and pepper. Cover, bring to a boil; simmer for 10 minutes.

Stir the lamb into the vegetable mixture. Cover and bake in a 350° oven for 1 hour, or until tender. Serve with garlic bread.

4 to 6 servings

Illustrated on page 31

Lamb Biriani

1 green chili pepper
1½ lb boneless lamb
  shoulder
2½ cups beef broth
  or water
2 tablespoons
  chopped coriander
2-inch piece fresh
  ginger, sliced
1 cinnamon stick
1 green pepper,
  seeded and
  quartered
Salt and pepper
4 onions
4 tablespoons butter
½ teaspoon each
  ground cardamom
  and cloves
1 teaspoon ground
  cinnamon
1 cup long-grain rice
¼ cup seedless
  raisins
½ teaspoon ground
  turmeric
2 teaspoons each
  ground coriander
  and cumin
8 cloves garlic,
  chopped
½ cup blanched
  almonds
¼ cup shelled
  pistachio nuts

Cut the chili lengthwise into quarters, removing the seeds.

Put the lamb, broth, chopped coriander, ginger, cinnamon stick, chili and green pepper into a flameproof 3-quart casserole. Add salt and pepper. Bring to the boil, cover and simmer for 1½ hours, or until the lamb is tender. Drain, reserving the stock. Cut the lamb into bite-size pieces and set aside.

Cut the onions into quarters and separate the layers. Melt the butter and allow to settle; then pour the clear liquid into a 10-inch skillet; do not add the milky residue. Add the onions to the skillet and sauté over high heat for 3 to 4 minutes, until very lightly browned. Remove the onions from the skillet; add the lamb and brown, together with the cardamom, cloves and ground cinnamon. Push to one side of the pan. Add the rice, raisins, turmeric, ground coriander, cumin and garlic; stir-fry a few minutes.

Strain the reserved stock, measure and add water to make 1½ cups. Add the stock and onions to the skillet, bring to a boil and simmer for 25 minutes. Adjust the seasoning.

Discard the cinnamon stick and stir in the nuts. Cover and let stand for 5 minutes before serving with traditional Indian accompaniments of fried onion rings, hard-cooked eggs, green pepper rings and sliced tomatoes.
4 servings

Moussaka

2 medium eggplants, sliced
Salt and pepper
6 tablespoons olive oil
1 large onion, chopped
1 clove garlic, finely chopped
3 cups finely chopped cooked lamb
1 can (8 oz) tomato sauce
2 tablespoons chopped parsley
Grated nutmeg
2 tablespoons butter
¼ cup flour
1½ cups milk
1 egg yolk

Sprinkle the eggplant slices with salt and let stand for 30 minutes. Rinse and pat dry with paper towels. Heat a little of the olive oil in a 10-inch skillet. Sauté the eggplant, a few slices at a time, until golden on both sides, adding oil as necessary.

Add the onion and garlic to the skillet and sauté until softened. Stir in the lamb, tomato sauce, parsley, salt, pepper and nutmeg. Simmer for about 5 minutes.

Line a 3-quart casserole with eggplant, pour in the lamb mixture and top with eggplant.

Melt the butter in a saucepan. Add the flour and cook, stirring, for 1 minute. Gradually stir in the milk and bring to a boil; simmer, stirring, until thickened. Season with salt, pepper and nutmeg to taste. Cool slightly, then beat in the egg yolk.

Pour the sauce over the eggplant. Bake in a 350° oven for 45 minutes. Serve with rice or a cracked wheat pilaf.
4 servings

Liver and Bacon Casserole

1 large onion, sliced
2 medium apples,
    peeled, cored and
    sliced
1 cup sliced
    mushrooms
½ lb sliced bacon
1½ lb lamb's or calf's
    liver, sliced
Salt and pepper
1 cup beef broth
1 can (16 oz) whole
    tomatoes, drained
    and chopped

Spread one-third of the onion over the bottom of a greased 3-quart casserole. Add one-third of the apple slices, then one-third of the mushrooms and bacon, then half the liver. Season well. Continue making layers in this way. Pour in the beef broth and spread the tomatoes on top.

Cover tightly and bake in a 350° oven for 1½ hours. Garnish with finely chopped parsley, if desired, and serve with boiled new potatoes.

4 servings

Lamb Chops and Apples

2 tablespoons butter
1 tablespoon oil
1 large onion, thinly sliced
2 large apples, peeled and sliced
2 tablespoons raisins
2 tablespoons brown sugar
Salt and pepper
8 shoulder lamb chops
⅔ cup cider

Melt the butter with the oil in a 12-inch skillet. Add the onion and sauté until soft. Remove the onion from the pan and spread half over the bottom of a shallow 3-quart baking dish. Cover with half the apples and sprinkle with half the raisins and half the sugar. Add salt and pepper.

Put the chops in the skillet and brown on both sides. Drain the chops and place in the baking dish. Cover with the remaining onion and apples and sprinkle with the remaining raisins and sugar. Add salt and pepper and pour in the cider.

Cover the baking dish with foil and bake in a 350° oven for 1½ hours, or until the chops are tender. Serve with curried rice (page 86).

4 servings

Lamb, Pork and Potato Bake

3 tablespoons butter
4 or 5 potatoes,
    sliced
1 lb boneless stewing
    lamb, cut into
    cubes
1 lb boneless pork,
    cut into cubes
2 onions, chopped
Salt and pepper
⅔ cup dry white
    wine

Grease a 3-quart baking dish with half the butter. Make a layer of half the potatoes on the bottom, then add the lamb and pork cubes and onions in layers, sprinkling each layer with a little salt and pepper. Pour in the wine. Arrange the remaining potatoes on top and dot with the remaining butter. Cover and bake in a 375° oven for 1½ hours.

Uncover the baking dish and continue baking for 30 minutes, or until the potato topping is golden brown. Serve with stir-fried shredded cabbage.
4 servings

Lamb and Mushroom Casserole

3 tablespoons butter
½ lb mushrooms, chopped
2 tablespoons flour
½ cup milk
¾ cup chicken broth
2 tablespoons dry sherry
Salt and pepper
3 cups chopped cooked lamb
1 lb tomatoes, sliced
½ cup soft bread crumbs
¼ cup shredded Cheddar cheese
2 tablespoons chopped parsley

Melt the butter in a 10-inch skillet. Add the mushrooms and sauté for 3 minutes. Sprinkle in the flour and cook, stirring, for 2 minutes. Gradually stir in the milk and broth. Bring to a boil and simmer, stirring, until thickened. Add the sherry, salt and pepper, then fold in the lamb. Pour into a greased 3-quart baking dish.

Arrange the tomato slices over the lamb mixture. Combine the bread crumbs, cheese and parsley and sprinkle over the top. Bake in a 350° oven for 30 minutes, or until the top is golden brown. Serve with garlic bread.
4 servings

Lamb and Bean Casserole

1 lb dried navy
  beans, soaked
  overnight
1 onion, stuck with
  4 cloves
1 bay leaf
3 tablespoons flour
Salt and pepper
2 lb boneless stewing
  lamb, cut into
  cubes
3 tablespoons oil
1 large onion,
  chopped
2 cloves garlic, finely
  chopped
1 can (16 oz) whole
  tomatoes, drained
  and chopped
2 cups chicken broth
1 tablespoon lemon
  juice
1 teaspoon dried
  thyme
⅓ cup dry bread
  crumbs
2 tablespoons butter,
  melted

Drain the beans and put them in a saucepan with the onion stuck with cloves and the bay leaf. Add fresh water to cover and bring to a boil. Simmer for 1 hour, or until the beans are tender.

Meanwhile, season the flour with salt and pepper and use to coat the lamb cubes. Heat the oil in a 4-quart Dutch oven, add the chopped onion and garlic and sauté until softened. Add the lamb and brown on all sides. Stir in the tomatoes, broth, lemon juice and thyme and bring to a boil. Cover and bake in a 350° oven for 1 hour.

Drain the beans, discarding the whole onion and bay leaf, and stir into the pot. Add a little more broth if necessary. Cover and bake 1 hour, or until the lamb is tender.

Mix together the bread crumbs and butter. Uncover the pot and sprinkle the bread crumbs on top. Bake for 15 to 20 minutes, or until the topping is golden brown. If desired, serve with a green salad and crusty bread.

4 to 6 servings

NOTE: No time to soak the beans? Here's a shortcut. Put them in a saucepan, cover with water and bring to a boil. Boil for 1 or 2 minutes, then turn off the heat and allow to stand for 1 hour. They are now ready to continue cooking.

VEAL

Braised Sweetbreads

1 pair sweetbreads
(1 lb)
2 tablespoons butter
1 medium onion,
finely chopped
1 large carrot,
chopped
1 stalk celery, finely
chopped
4 slices cooked ham,
cut into strips
⅔ cup chicken broth
⅔ cup dry white
wine
Salt and pepper

Blanch the sweetbreads in acidulated boiling water (1 tablespoon lemon juice or vinegar for each quart of water) for 10 minutes. Drain, then remove the veins and membranes. Cut into slices.

Melt the butter in a 1½-quart flameproof casserole. Add the onion, carrot, celery and ham and sauté until the onion is softened. Stir in the broth, wine, salt and pepper. Bring to a boil. Arrange the sweetbreads on top of the vegetables, cover and bake in a 375° oven for 30 minutes. Serve with crisp toast or rice and celery au gratin.
4 servings

Braised Sweetbreads;
Veal Goulash (page 42);
Veal and Pork Casserole

Veal and Pork Casserole

1 lb boneless stewing veal, cut into cubes

1 lb boneless pork, cut into cubes

Chicken broth or water

8 oz noodles

Salt and pepper

1 can (10¾ oz) condensed cream of chicken soup, undiluted

3 cups grated Cheddar cheese

1 can (12 oz) whole kernel corn, drained

1 cup soft bread crumbs

Put the veal and pork cubes in a saucepan and add broth to cover. Bring to a boil, skimming off any scum that rises to the surface. Simmer for 45 minutes.

Meanwhile, cook the noodles in boiling salted water until just tender. Drain and mix with the soup, 2 cups of the cheese, salt and pepper.

Drain the veal and pork and add to the noodle mixture. Stir well and spoon into a 3-quart baking dish.

Spread the corn over the meat and noodle mixture. Combine the bread crumbs with the remaining cheese and scatter over the top. Bake in a 350° oven for 20 to 30 minutes, or until the top is browned. Serve with a green salad.

4 to 6 servings

Veal Goulash

2 slices bacon
2 tablespoons butter
1 medium onion, chopped
1 cup sliced mushrooms
2 lb boneless stewing veal, cut into cubes
½ teaspoon paprika
1 cup sour cream
⅔ cup beef broth or water
Salt and pepper

Fry the bacon in a 10-inch skillet. Drain on paper towels, crumble and place in a 3-quart casserole. Add the butter and onion to the skillet and sauté until golden. Stir in the mushrooms and sauté for 5 minutes longer. Transfer with a slotted spoon to the casserole.

Add the veal cubes to the skillet and brown on all sides. As the veal browns, transfer to the casserole.

Stir the paprika into the fat in the skillet and cook for 2 minutes. Stir in the sour cream, broth, salt and pepper. Pour into the casserole and stir. Cover and cook in a 325° oven for 1 hour, or until the meat is tender. Sprinkle with paprika, if desired, and serve with rice or noodles.

4 servings

Veal Parmesan

½ cup dry bread crumbs
¼ cup grated Parmesan cheese
Salt and pepper
1 lb veal cutlets, cut into pieces
1 egg, beaten
4 tablespoons butter, melted
2 tablespoons olive oil
1 onion, thinly sliced
1 can (16 oz) crushed tomatoes
2 tablespoons tomato paste
½ teaspoon sugar
½ teaspoon dried oregano

Mix together the bread crumbs and the cheese, salt and pepper. Dip the veal into the beaten egg, then coat with the crumb mixture.

Pour the melted butter into a 2-quart baking dish and arrange the veal squares in the dish, in one layer, turning them to coat with the melted butter. Bake in a 400° oven for 20 minutes. Turn the veal and bake 15 minutes longer.

Meanwhile, heat the oil in a saucepan and sauté the onion until soft. Add the tomatoes, tomato paste, sugar and oregano. Simmer until well reduced. Add salt and pepper to taste.

Pour the tomato sauce over the veal and continue baking for 5 to 10 minutes. If desired, garnish with chopped parsley.

4 servings   Illustrated on pages 40-41

Veal with Orange

2 tablespoons butter
1 tablespoon oil
1½ lb boneless
  stewing veal, cut
  into cubes
1 onion, sliced
3 tablespoons flour
1¼ cups chicken
  broth
⅔ cup orange juice
Salt and pepper
2 oranges, peeled and
  sliced

Melt the butter with the oil in a 10-inch skillet. Add the veal cubes and brown on all sides. Transfer with a slotted spoon to a 2-quart baking dish.

Add the onion to the skillet and sauté until golden brown. Add to the casserole.

Stir the flour into the fat remaining in the skillet and cook for 3 minutes. Gradually stir in the broth and orange juice and bring to a boil. Season with salt and pepper and pour over the veal. Arrange the orange slices, overlapping, on top.

Cover with foil and bake in a 350° oven for 1½ to 2 hours, or until the veal is tender. If desired, garnish with watercress and serve with curried rice (page 86).

4 servings

Meatball Casserole

2 lb ground veal
¼ cup soft bread crumbs
2 tablespoons grated Parmesan cheese
2 tablespoons chopped parsley
Salt and pepper
1 egg, beaten
2 tablespoons butter
1 tablespoon oil
1 onion, chopped
2 stalks celery, chopped
1 apple, peeled and diced
¾ cup chicken broth
½ cup dry red wine
¼ cup sweet pickle relish
2 tablespoons chopped raisins

Mix together the veal, bread crumbs, cheese, parsley, salt and pepper. Bind the mixture with the egg. Shape into meatballs about the size of walnuts.

Melt the butter with the oil in a 10-inch skillet. Add the meatballs, a few at a time, and brown on all sides, then transfer to a 3-quart casserole.

Add the onion, celery and apple to the skillet and sauté until the onion is softened. Stir in the broth, wine, relish and raisins and bring to a boil. Simmer for 10 minutes.

Pour the sauce over the meatballs. Cover and bake in a 375° oven for 30 minutes, or until the meatballs are cooked through. If desired, garnish with chopped parsley and serve with scalloped potatoes (see page 77) and a green vegetable.

4 to 6 servings

Roman Veal Casserole

¼ cup flour
Salt and pepper
2 lb veal cutlets, cut into pieces
2 tablespoons butter
1 tablespoon olive oil
½ lb mushrooms, sliced
1 clove garlic, chopped
1 can (16 oz) whole tomatoes, drained and chopped
⅔ cup Marsala
1 teaspoon dried basil or rosemary or 1 tablespoon fresh
½ teaspoon dried oregano

Season the flour with salt and pepper and use to coat the veal. Melt the butter with the oil in a flameproof 3-quart casserole. Add the veal and brown, then remove and set aside.

Add the mushrooms and garlic to the casserole and sauté for 3 minutes. Stir in the tomatoes, Marsala and herbs. Season to taste with salt and pepper. Bring to a boil.

Return the veal to the casserole and mix into the sauce. Cover and bake in a 325° oven for 45 minutes. Garnish with parsley, if desired, and serve with cornbread.

4 servings

FISH & SHELLFISH

Mediterranean Fish Steaks

¼ cup olive oil
2 onions, sliced
1 clove garlic,
  chopped
1 green pepper,
  seeded and sliced
  into rings
4 large tomatoes,
  sliced
2 teaspoons dried
  basil
Salt and pepper
4 fish steaks
  (halibut,
  swordfish, cod)
2 teaspoons lemon
  juice
6 tablespoons dry
  white wine

Heat the oil in a 10-inch skillet and sauté the onions and garlic until soft. Add the green pepper rings and continue cooking for 3 minutes. Remove from the heat and place half the mixture in a 2-quart baking dish.

Arrange half the tomatoes on top and sprinkle with half the basil and salt and pepper. Place the fish steaks on top and sprinkle with the lemon juice. Add the remaining tomatoes, basil and onion and green pepper mixture. Pour in the wine.

Cover and bake in a 350° oven for about 45 minutes, or until the fish is tender. Serve with buttered boiled potatoes.

4 servings

Greek Shrimp Casserole

1¼ cups water
Juice of ½ lemon
2 lb shrimp
3 tablespoons olive oil
1 onion, finely chopped
1 clove garlic, chopped
2 cans (16 oz each) whole tomatoes, drained and chopped
¾ teaspoon dried oregano
Salt and pepper
¾ cup crumbled feta cheese

Bring the water and lemon juice to a boil in a saucepan. Add the shrimp and simmer for 5 minutes, or until pink. Drain, reserving the liquid. Cool shrimp slightly, then peel and devein. Reduce the liquid to ⅔ cup.

Heat the oil in a 10-inch skillet. Add the onion and garlic and sauté until soft. Stir in the tomatoes, oregano and reserved cooking liquid. Simmer until the sauce is reduced and thickened. Add salt and pepper to taste.

Fold the shrimp into the sauce. Transfer to a 1½-quart baking dish. Sprinkle the cheese on top and bake in a 350° oven for 15 minutes. Serve with rice.

4 servings

Mornay Fillets

1 lb spinach
Salt and pepper
4 tablespoons butter
1 cup sliced
  mushrooms
1½ lb red snapper
  fillets
5 tablespoons flour
2 cups milk
½ cup grated Swiss
  cheese
½ cup grated
  Cheddar cheese
Grated nutmeg

Steam the spinach, with only the water clinging to the leaves after washing, until just wilted. Drain well, squeezing out excess water, then chop. Season with salt and pepper and stir in 1 tablespoon of the butter. Spread the spinach in the bottom of a greased 2-quart baking dish. Cover with the mushrooms and arrange the fish fillets on top.

Melt the remaining butter in a saucepan. Add the flour and cook, stirring, for 1 minute. Gradually stir in the milk and bring to a boil. Simmer, stirring, until thickened. Stir in all but 2 tablespoons of the cheese, and season to taste with salt, pepper and nutmeg.

Pour the cheese sauce over the fish and sprinkle the reserved cheese on top. Bake in a 350° oven for about 30 minutes, or until the fish is cooked. Garnish with parsley, if desired, and serve with noodles.

4 servings

Shellfish Casserole

4 to 6 potatoes
Salt and pepper
3 tablespoons butter
2 tablespoons flour
¾ cup milk
¾ cup dry white
  wine
1 can (6½ oz)
  crabmeat, drained
  and flaked
1½ lb shrimp, peeled
  and deveined
1 small onion, grated
3 tablespoons
  chopped parsley
¾ cup shredded
  Cheddar cheese

Parboil the potatoes in boiling salted water for 10 minutes, then drain and slice thinly.

Melt 2 tablespoons of the butter in a saucepan. Add the flour and cook, stirring, for 1 minute. Gradually stir in the milk and wine and bring to a boil. Simmer, stirring, until thickened. Add salt and pepper and fold in the remaining ingredients.

Layer one-third of the potato slices in a greased 2-quart baking dish. Cover with half the shellfish mixture. Repeat the layers, finishing with a layer of potato slices. Dot with the remaining butter.

Bake in a 350° oven for about 45 minutes, or until the potatoes are tender and the top is golden. If desired, garnish with watercress and serve with a green salad.

4 servings

Fish Boulangère

4 medium potatoes
Salt and pepper
4 tablespoons butter
1 clove of garlic,
   finely chopped
1½ lb flounder
   fillets, cut into
   chunks
1 large onion, thinly
   sliced

Parboil the potatoes in boiling salted water for 10 minutes, then drain and slice thinly.

Cream half the butter with the garlic and spread in the bottom of a 2-quart baking dish. Arrange the fish on top and sprinkle with salt and pepper. Cover with the onion and then the potato. Dot with the remaining butter.

Bake in a 350° oven for about 40 minutes, or until the potatoes are tender. Serve with broiled tomatoes or a cucumber salad.

4 servings

Haddock with Grapefruit

4 haddock fillets
   (1½ lb)
4 tablespoons butter
3 green onions,
   thinly sliced
Salt and pepper
2 grapefruit
½ lb mushrooms,
   sliced

Arrange the haddock fillets in a greased casserole. Mash the butter with the green onions, salt and pepper. Grate the rind from the grapefruit and mix with the butter. Spread over the haddock fillets. Cover with the mushrooms.

Squeeze the juice from one grapefruit; peel and segment the other. Pour the grapefruit juice over the mushrooms and place the grapefruit segments on top.

Cover and bake in a 350° oven for about 30 minutes, or until the fish is cooked. Serve with rice.

4 servings

Tuna Noodle Casserole

4 cups noodles
Salt and pepper
1 can (10¾ oz)
    condensed cream
    of mushroom
    soup, undiluted
2 tablespoons dry
    sherry
2 cans (7 oz each)
    tuna, drained and
    flaked
6 green onions,
    thinly sliced
4 hard-cooked eggs,
    sliced
½ cup crushed
    potato chips
2 tablespoons grated
    Parmesan cheese

Cook the noodles in boiling salted water until just tender. Drain, then mix in the soup and sherry. Put about one-third of the noodle mixture in a greased 3-quart casserole. Cover with half the tuna, green onions and eggs; season with salt and pepper. Repeat the layers and top with the remaining noodle mixture.

Mix together the potato chips and cheese and sprinkle over the top. Bake in a 350° oven for 25 to 30 minutes, or until the top is golden brown. Serve with a tray of raw vegetables.

4 to 6 servings

Haddock in Cider

1½ lb haddock
    fillets, cut into
    chunks
2 apples, cored and
    sliced
2 stalks celery,
    chopped
¼ teaspoon dried
    sage
Salt and pepper
1¼ cups cider
1 tablespoon butter
2 tablespoons flour

Put the fish in a greased 12 × 7½-inch baking dish and cover with the apple slices and celery. Sprinkle with the sage, salt and pepper, then pour in the cider.

Cover with foil and bake in a 350° oven for 25 to 35 minutes, or until the fish is cooked.

Transfer the fish and apples to a warmed serving dish and keep hot.

Blend the butter with the flour to make a smooth paste. Place in a saucepan and add a little of the hot cooking liquid. Stir in the remaining cooking liquid in the baking dish. Bring to a boil, stirring, and simmer until thickened; pour over the fish and garnish with parsley if desired.

4 servings

Crab and Spaghetti Bake

8 oz thin spaghetti
Salt and pepper
2 tablespoons butter
1 large onion,
  chopped
1 sweet red pepper,
  seeded and diced
3 tablespoons flour
1¼ cups milk
½ cup half-and-half
2 teaspoons Dijon
  mustard
1 tablespoon
  Worcestershire
  sauce
2 cans (6½ oz)
  crabmeat, drained
  and flaked
4 hard-cooked eggs,
  sliced
1 cup shredded sharp
  Cheddar cheese

Break the spaghetti into short lengths and cook in boiling salted water until just tender.

Meanwhile, melt the butter in a large saucepan, add the onion and red pepper and sauté until softened. Stir in the flour and cook, stirring, for 1 minute, then gradually stir in the milk and half-and-half. Bring to a boil and simmer, stirring, until thickened. Stir in the mustard, Worcestershire, salt and pepper.

Drain the spaghetti and fold into the sauce. Spread half this mixture in a greased 3-quart baking dish. Cover with the crabmeat, then the sliced eggs and top with the remaining spaghetti mixture. Sprinkle the cheese over the top. Bake in a 375° oven for 25 minutes, or until heated through and bubbling. Serve with a spinach salad if desired.

4 servings

POULTRY

Almond Chicken Curry

1 tablespoon oil
2 onions, chopped
1 clove garlic,
  chopped
1 tablespoon curry
  powder (see note)
2 lb chicken parts,
  skinned
2 teaspoons tomato
  paste
¼ cup lemon juice
1 bay leaf
1¼ cups chicken
  broth
¼ cup slivered
  almonds, toasted

Heat the oil in a 10-inch skillet, add the onions and garlic and sauté gently until soft. Stir in the curry powder and sauté for 5 minutes, stirring. Add the chicken pieces and brown on all sides. Add the tomato paste, lemon juice, bay leaf and broth. Bring to a boil, cover and simmer for about 40 minutes.

Discard the bay leaf. Sprinkle the chicken with the almonds and serve with rice and curry condiments.
4 servings

NOTE: Curry powder can be added to taste.

Florida Chicken Drumsticks

3 tablespoons oil
8 chicken
    drumsticks
½ package (2¼-oz
    size) asparagus
    soup mix
1¼ cups boiling
    water
1 small onion, cut
    into 8 pieces
1 package (10 oz)
    frozen cut green
    beans
Salt and pepper
1 avocado
½ cup crushed
    potato chips

Heat the oil in a 10-inch skillet, add the drumsticks and brown on all sides. Sprinkle in the soup mix, stir in the boiling water and add the onion. Cook over moderate heat for about 3 to 4 minutes, until thickened. Cover and simmer for 15 minutes.

Stir in the beans, add salt and pepper, cover and continue simmering 10 minutes longer, or until the chicken is tender.

Cut the avocado into 12 sections and arrange over the chicken. Cover and heat for 2 or 3 minutes.

Sprinkle with the crushed potato chips and serve with rice.

4 servings

Coq au Vin

¼ lb salt pork, diced
1 chicken (3 to 3½ lb), cut into pieces
½ lb small white onions
1 clove garlic, chopped
2 tablespoons flour
2½ cups dry red wine
Salt and pepper
½ lb small mushrooms
⅔ cup chicken broth
Bouquet garni

Blanch the salt pork in boiling water for 5 minutes, then drain. Sauté the pork in a 10-inch skillet until crisp. Remove with a slotted spoon and place in a 3-quart casserole.

Add the chicken pieces to the skillet and brown on all sides; transfer to the casserole.

Add the onions and garlic to the skillet and cook gently until they begin to soften and brown. Add to the casserole.

Pour off all but about 2 tablespoons of fat from the skillet and stir in the flour. Cook, stirring, for 2 minutes. Gradually stir in the wine and bring to a boil, then simmer, stirring, until thickened. Season with salt and pepper and stir in the mushrooms.

Pour the sauce over the chicken in the casserole, adding enough broth to cover. Add the bouquet garni, cover and bake in a 375° oven for about 1 hour, or until the chicken is tender. Remove the bouquet garni. Garnish with chopped parsley, if desired, and serve with French bread.

4 servings

Arroz con Pollo

4 tablespoons butter
3 tablespoons olive
  oil
1 clove garlic,
  chopped
1 chicken (3 to
  3½ lb), cut into
  pieces
2 cups long-grain
  rice
4 cups chicken broth
1 teaspoon turmeric
Salt and pepper
¼ lb chorizo or garlic
  sausage, chopped
1 sweet red pepper,
  seeded and diced

Melt the butter with the oil in a 3-quart flameproof casserole. Add the garlic and chicken pieces and brown on all sides. Remove the chicken.

Add the rice to the casserole and stir to coat with the fat. Sauté until golden, stirring, then stir in the broth, turmeric, salt and pepper. Bring to a boil.

Add the chorizo and red pepper and mix. Return the chicken pieces to the casserole and bury in the rice mixture. Cover and bake in a 350° oven for about 1 hour, or until the chicken is tender and the rice has absorbed the liquid. Garnish with parsley if desired.

4 to 6 servings

Curried Chicken Casserole

4 tablespoons butter
2 large onions, finely
  chopped
1 clove garlic,
  chopped
1 green chili pepper,
  seeded and finely
  chopped
1 inch gingerroot,
  finely chopped
1 teaspoon turmeric
1 teaspoon each
  ground coriander
  and cumin
½ teaspoon ground
  cardamom
1 teaspoon salt
2 cups plain yogurt
2½ lb chicken parts,
  skinned

Melt the butter in a 3-quart flameproof casserole, add the onions and sauté until soft. Stir in the garlic, chili pepper, ginger, turmeric, coriander, cumin, cardamom and salt and cook, stirring, for 5 minutes. Stir in the yogurt, then add the chicken to the casserole and spoon the yogurt mixture over them.

Cover and bake in a 325° oven for 1¼ hours, or until the chicken is tender. Serve with noodles.

4 servings

Spring Chicken Casserole

3 tablespoons flour
Salt and pepper
1 chicken (3 to
3½ lb), cut into
pieces
4 tablespoons butter
8 small carrots
12 small white
onions
1 stalk celery, cut
into 2-inch pieces
2 cups boiling
chicken broth
Bouquet garni
3 tablespoons heavy
cream

Season the flour with a little salt and pepper, then use to coat the chicken. Melt the butter in a skillet and brown the chicken on all sides. Transfer to a 3-quart casserole.

Add the carrots, onions and celery to the fat in the skillet and sauté until just golden. Add to the chicken in the casserole. Pour in the broth and add the bouquet garni.

Cover and bake in a 350° oven for about 1¼ hours, or until the chicken and vegetables are tender. Discard the bouquet garni. Stir in the cream and heat through. Serve with rice or boiled new potatoes, if desired.

4 servings

Chicken and Leek Casserole

1 lb leeks
2 cups diced cooked
    chicken
5 tablespoons butter
6 tablespoons flour
1 cup chicken broth
1¼ cups milk
¼ teaspoon dry
    mustard
Salt and pepper
¾ cup shredded
    Cheddar cheese
⅓ cup dry bread
    crumbs

Halve the leeks crosswise, then cut into quarters lengthwise. Wash thoroughly. Place in a greased 2-quart casserole with the chicken on top.

Melt 4 tablespoons of the butter in a saucepan. Add the flour and cook, stirring, for 2 minutes. Gradually stir in the broth and milk. Bring to a boil, then simmer, stirring, until thickened. Add the mustard, salt and pepper to taste and the cheese; stir until melted. Pour over the chicken and leeks.

Melt the remaining butter and mix with the bread crumbs. Scatter over the top of the casserole. Bake in a 350° oven for 30 minutes.

4 servings

Illustrated above:
Chicken and Leek Casserole;
Grapefruit Chicken (page 62)

Grapefruit Chicken

4 whole chicken
  breasts, skinned
  and halved
Salt and pepper
2 tablespoons butter
1 tablespoon oil
1 large onion, sliced
1 teaspoon grated
  grapefruit rind
¾ cup grapefruit
  juice
3 tablespoons honey
Grapefruit segments

Rub the chicken breasts with salt and pepper. Melt the butter with the oil in a 10-inch skillet and sauté the chicken pieces until browned. Transfer to a 3-quart casserole.

Add the onion to the fat remaining in the skillet and sauté until soft. Arrange the onion over the chicken.

Mix together the grapefruit rind and juice, honey, salt and pepper, then pour over the chicken. Cover and bake in a 350° oven for about 1 hour, or until the chicken is cooked through. Garnish with grapefruit segments. Serve with curried rice (page 86).

4 to 6 servings

Illustrated on page 61

Smothered Chicken

½ cup flour
Salt and pepper
1 chicken (3 to
  3½ lb), cut into
  pieces
4 tablespoons butter
1 onion, finely
  chopped
1 small carrot, diced
1 stalk celery, finely
  chopped
2 cups chicken broth
6 tablespoons heavy
  cream or
  half-and-half

Season half the flour with salt and pepper and use to coat the chicken pieces. Melt the butter in a 10-inch skillet and brown the chicken on all sides. Transfer to a 3-quart casserole.

Add the onion, carrot and celery to the fat remaining in the skillet and sauté until the onion is softened. Sprinkle in the remaining flour and cook, stirring, for 3 minutes. Gradually stir in the broth and bring to a boil. Simmer, stirring, until thickened, then pour over the chicken.

Cover and bake in a 350° oven for about 1 hour, or until the chicken is tender.

Transfer the chicken to a warmed serving dish and keep hot. Stir the cream into the sauce in the casserole and adjust the seasoning. Pour over the chicken. If desired, serve with pearl barley casserole (page 90).

4 servings

Citrus Chicken

1 chicken (3 to
  3½ lb), quartered
Salt and pepper
Ground cinnamon
2 large lemons or
  limes
2 large oranges
2 tablespoons butter

Rub the chicken pieces with salt, pepper and a little cinnamon. Place in a greased 3-quart casserole.

Squeeze the juice from one of the lemons or limes and pour over the chicken. Grate the rind from one of the oranges. Peel the remaining lemon or lime and both oranges, and chop the flesh. Mix the chopped fruit with the grated orange rind and spread over the chicken. Dot with the butter.

Cover tightly and bake in a 375° oven for 1 hour, or until tender. Garnish with parsley if desired.

4 servings

Chicken in Sour Cream

4 tablespoons butter
1 cup sliced
   mushrooms
¼ cup flour
⅔ cup dry white
   wine
1¼ cups milk or
   half-and-half
⅔ cup sour cream
Grated nutmeg
Salt and pepper
4 whole chicken
   breasts, boned,
   skinned and
   halved

Melt the butter in a 2-quart saucepan, add the mushrooms and sauté until just tender. Remove from the pan with a slotted spoon and set aside.

Add the flour to the fat remaining in the pan and cook, stirring, for 1 minute. Gradually stir in the wine and milk; bring to a boil and simmer, stirring, until thickened. Add half the mushrooms, the sour cream, and season with nutmeg, salt and pepper.

Arrange the chicken breasts in a shallow 3-quart casserole. Pour the sauce over them. Cover and bake in a 350° oven for about 40 minutes, or until tender. Garnish with the remaining mushrooms and chopped parsley, if desired, and serve with green peppers and beans (page 74) and boiled or mashed potatoes.

4 to 8 servings

Spicy Chicken with Fruit

3 tablespoons flour
Salt and pepper
1 chicken (3 to
   3½ lb), quartered
4 tablespoons butter
1 onion, thinly sliced
1 tablespoon chili
   powder (or more,
   to taste)
1 can (8¼ oz) whole
   tomatoes
½ cup chicken broth
2 fresh peaches,
   peeled and sliced
3 bananas, thinly
   sliced

Season the flour with salt and pepper and use to coat the chicken. Melt the butter in a 10-inch skillet and brown the chicken on all sides; transfer to a shallow 3-quart casserole.

Add the onion to the skillet and sauté until softened. Stir in the chili powder, tomatoes with their juice and broth. Bring to a boil. Season with salt and pepper and stir in the peaches and bananas. Pour this mixture over the chicken.

Cover and bake in a 350° oven for 1¼ to 1½ hours, or until the chicken is tender. If desired, serve with curried rice (page 86).

4 servings

Chicken Pilaf

4 tablespoons butter
¼ cup flour
1 can (13 oz) evaporated milk
1½ cups chicken broth
2 cups diced cooked chicken
3 cups cooked rice
1 cup sliced mushrooms
1 small green pepper, seeded and chopped
1 small sweet red pepper, seeded and chopped
Salt and pepper

Melt the butter in a 3-quart saucepan. Add the flour and cook, stirring, for 2 minutes. Gradually stir in the evaporated milk and broth and bring to a boil. Simmer, stirring, until thickened.

Fold in the chicken, rice, mushrooms, peppers and salt and pepper to taste. Reduce heat and simmer 5 minutes. Or, spoon into a greased 2-quart casserole. Bake in a 350° oven for 30 minutes, or until heated through. Serve with a salad.

6 servings

Crispy Chicken

2 cups diced cooked chicken
4 stalks celery, chopped
⅔ cup mayonnaise
2 tablespoons lemon juice
4 green onions, finely sliced
¼ cup slivered almonds, toasted
½ cup shredded Cheddar cheese
Salt and pepper
½ cup crushed potato chips

Mix together the chicken, celery, mayonnaise, lemon juice, green onions, almonds, cheese, salt and pepper. Spoon into a 1½-quart casserole. Sprinkle the potato chips over the top and cook in a 400° oven for 25 to 30 minutes, or until piping hot.

4 servings

Turkey Bake

2 cups diced cooked
   turkey
2 medium potatoes,
   cooked and diced
1 onion, grated
¾ cup milk
1 egg, beaten
1 teaspoon grated
   lemon rind
Salt and pepper
12 saltines, finely
   crushed
1 tablespoon butter,
   melted

Mix together the turkey, potatoes, onion, milk, egg, lemon rind and salt and pepper to taste. Spoon into a greased shallow 2-quart casserole.

Combine the crushed saltines and melted butter and sprinkle over the top. Bake in a 350° oven for about 30 minutes. Serve with a mixed salad.

4 servings

Turkey and Rice Amandine

3 tablespoons butter
3 stalks celery,
   chopped
1 large onion,
   chopped
½ lb mushrooms,
   sliced
1 cup long-grain rice
1 jar (2 oz) chopped
   pimiento, drained
1 can (10¾ oz)
   condensed cream
   of celery soup,
   undiluted
1½ cups water
2 cups slivered
   cooked turkey
2 cups slivered
   almonds
Salt and pepper
½ cup shredded
   Cheddar cheese

Melt the butter in a skillet. Add the celery, onion and mushrooms and sauté until softened. Transfer to a greased 2-quart casserole. Add the rice, pimiento, soup, water, turkey, half of the almonds, salt and pepper, and stir until well combined. Top with the remaining almonds and sprinkle with the cheese.

Cover and bake in a 325° oven for 50 minutes. Uncover and bake 20 minutes longer, or until the top is golden and the rice is tender.

4 servings

Turkey Tetrazzini

8 oz thin spaghetti
Salt and pepper
5 tablespoons butter
¼ cup flour
2½ cups chicken broth
1 cup milk or half-and-half
½ cup dry white wine
1 teaspoon dry mustard
1 cup grated Parmesan cheese
½ lb mushrooms, sliced
3 cups diced cooked turkey

Cook the spaghetti in boiling salted water until just tender. Drain and place in a greased 2-quart casserole.

Meanwhile, melt 2 tablespoons of the butter in a 3-quart saucepan, add the flour and cook, stirring, for 1 minute. Gradually stir in the broth, milk, wine, mustard, salt and pepper, and cook, stirring, until thickened. Remove from the heat and stir in three-quarters of the cheese. Pour the sauce over the spaghetti and stir well. Melt the remaining 3 tablespoons of butter in a skillet and sauté the mushrooms until tender. Add the mushrooms and turkey to the casserole.

Top with the remaining cheese and bake in a 375° oven for 20 to 25 minutes, or until lightly browned.
6 servings

VEGETABLES

Tomatoes in Sherry Cream

8 large tomatoes,
   peeled and sliced
3 tablespoons dry
   sherry
½ teaspoon sugar
Salt and pepper
¼ cup grated
   Parmesan cheese
⅔ cup heavy cream

Arrange the tomatoes in a greased 3-quart baking dish. Sprinkle with the sherry, sugar, salt and pepper, then the Parmesan. Pour the cream over the top.

  Bake in a 400° oven for about 20 minutes. Garnish with parsley, if desired, and serve with an omelet and toast.

4 servings

Eggplant and Bacon Casserole;
Tomatoes in Sherry Cream;
Broccoli Lorraine (page 72)

Eggplant and Bacon Casserole

1 eggplant (1½ lb), cut into ½-inch slices
Salt and pepper
5 tablespoons oil
½ lb sliced bacon, diced
1 large onion, chopped
1 clove garlic, chopped
1 green pepper, seeded and diced
½ lb mushrooms, sliced
1 can (16 oz) whole tomatoes
½ teaspoon dried thyme
1 teaspoon sugar
1 cup shredded mozzarella or Swiss cheese

Sprinkle the eggplant slices with salt and let stand for 30 minutes. Rinse and pat dry.

Brush a baking sheet with oil and arrange the eggplant on top in a single layer. Brush with the remaining oil. Bake in a 450° oven for 35 minutes.

Meanwhile, sauté the bacon in a 10-inch skillet until crisp; drain on paper towels. Pour off all but 2 tablespoons of fat from the skillet.

Add the onion, garlic and green pepper and sauté until the onion is softened. Stir in the mushrooms, tomatoes with their juice, thyme, sugar, salt and pepper. Simmer until quite thick, stirring occasionally.

Layer the eggplant slices, bacon and tomato sauce in a shallow 3-quart baking dish. Top with the cheese. Bake in a 350° oven for 20 minutes, or until the cheese melts and begins to brown. Serve with rice or a crusty bread.

4 to 6 servings

Broccoli Lorraine

1½ lb broccoli, cut
   into 2-inch pieces
4 slices bacon, diced
1 onion, thinly sliced
1¼ cups milk
½ cup half-and-half
4 eggs, beaten
¼ cup grated
   Gruyère or Swiss
   cheese
Salt and pepper

Arrange the broccoli in a greased 2-quart casserole. Sauté the bacon in a skillet until crisp. Remove the bacon with a slotted spoon and sprinkle on top of the broccoli.

Sauté the onion in the bacon fat until golden; remove with a slotted spoon and scatter on the broccoli.

Mix the milk, half-and-half, eggs, cheese, salt and pepper; pour into the casserole.

Place the casserole in a roasting pan containing about 1 inch of boiling water. Bake in a 350° oven for 30 minutes, or until just set.

4 servings

NOTE: If you prefer, omit the half-and-half and use 1¾ cups milk.

Illustrated on page 71

Rutabaga and Apple Casserole

If you are tired of serving mashed turnips at Thanksgiving, try this switch for a change.

1½ lb rutabaga,
   cubed
Salt and pepper
1 large tart apple,
   peeled and sliced
⅓ cup packed brown
   sugar
3 tablespoons butter
3 to 4 tablespoons
   dry sherry
   (optional)

Cook the rutabaga in boiling salted water for 20 to 30 minutes, or until just tender. Drain.

Put half the rutabaga in a greased casserole and cover with half the apple slices. Sprinkle with half the brown sugar; add salt and pepper. Dot with half the butter. Repeat the layers. Sprinkle with the sherry.

Cover and bake in a 350° oven for 30 minutes.

4 servings

Pineapple Parsnips

2 lb parsnips,
 quartered
 lengthwise
Salt and pepper
⅔ cup unsweetened
 pineapple juice
3 tablespoons butter

Cut the cores from the parsnips, then place in a greased baking dish. Sprinkle with salt and pepper and pour in the pineapple juice. Dot with the butter. Cover and bake in a 350° oven for 1 hour, or until tender.

4 to 6 servings

Green Peppers and Beans

1 lb green beans
2 green peppers,
   seeded and
   chopped
2 medium onions,
   finely chopped
Salt and pepper
Dried thyme
3 tablespoons butter

If the beans are large, cut in half. Make alternate layers of the vegetables in a greased 1½-quart casserole, beginning and ending with the beans. Sprinkle each layer with salt, pepper and a little thyme and dot with butter.

Cover tightly and bake in a 350° oven for 1 hour, or until the vegetables are tender. Serve with grilled cheese sandwiches.

4 to 6 servings

Red Cabbage with Apple

8 cups shredded red
    cabbage (about
    2 lb)
3 tablespoons butter
1 onion, sliced
2 medium tart
    apples, peeled and
    sliced
3 tablespoons water
3 tablespoons wine
    vinegar
4 teaspoons sugar
Salt and pepper
2 tablespoons flour

Blanch the cabbage in boiling water for 1 minute, then drain well. Melt 2 tablespoons of the butter in a 1½-quart flameproof casserole. Add the onion and sauté until softened. Add the apples and sauté for 5 minutes more. Remove from the casserole with a slotted spoon.

Make alternate layers of the cabbage and apple mixture in the casserole, beginning and ending with cabbage. Sprinkle each layer with water, vinegar, sugar, salt and pepper. Cover tightly and bake in a 325° oven for 2 hours, stirring occasionally and adding water if necessary.

Blend the remaining butter with the flour to make a paste. Mix with a little of the cooking liquid, then stir it into the casserole. Cook gently on top of the range until thickened. Garnish with parsley if desired.

4 to 6 servings

Lima Beans with Walnuts

2 tablespoons butter
1 small onion, finely
    chopped
⅔ cup chicken broth
2 cups shredded
    Cheddar cheese
1½ teaspoons Dijon
    mustard
1 teaspoon
    Worcestershire
    sauce
Salt and pepper
2 packages (10 oz
    each) frozen lima
    beans, thawed
1 cup chopped
    walnuts

Melt the butter in a 3-quart saucepan. Add the onion and sauté until softened. Stir in the broth and bring to a boil. Add the cheese, stir until melted, then mix in the mustard, Worcestershire, salt and pepper. Fold in the beans and walnuts.

Pour into a greased 1½-quart baking dish. Bake in a 350° oven for about 30 minutes.

4 to 6 servings

Stuffed Cabbage

1 medium head
  Savoy cabbage
2 tablespoons olive
  oil
4 slices ham,
  chopped
1 onion, chopped
1 clove garlic,
  chopped
1 egg, beaten
2 tablespoons grated
  Parmesan cheese
3 tablespoons
  chopped parsley
Salt and pepper
1 cup chicken broth

Cook the whole cabbage in boiling
water for 15 minutes. Drain and cool
under cold running water. Cut out the
core, then remove the inner cabbage
leaves, leaving the outside leaves in-
tact. Chop the inner leaves.

Heat the oil in a 10-inch skillet, add
the chopped cabbage leaves, ham,
onion and garlic and sauté until the
onion is soft. Remove from the heat.
Mix together the egg, cheese and parsley and stir into the cabbage mixture.
Season to taste with salt and pepper.

Place the cabbage "shell" of large
outside leaves in a foil-lined casserole
and fill with the sautéed mixture. Pour
in the broth. Cover and bake in a 375°
oven for 1 hour; uncover and bake 30
minutes. To serve, lift the cabbage out
with the foil, then remove the foil.
6 to 8 servings

Scalloped Potatoes

2 lb potatoes, thinly
 sliced
1 onion, thinly sliced
6 tablespoons flour
Salt and pepper
2½ cups milk
¼ cup dry bread
 crumbs
1 tablespoon butter

Make a layer of about one-third of the potato slices in a greased 2-quart casserole. Sprinkle with one-third of the onion and flour and season with salt and pepper. Repeat these layers twice, then pour in the milk.

Mix the bread crumbs with the butter and sprinkle over the top. Cover and bake in a 350° oven for 1¼ hours.

Remove the cover and continue baking for 15 minutes, or until the potatoes are very tender and the top is crisp and brown. A delicious accompaniment for any roast meat.

6 to 8 servings

Corn Custard

1 can (12 oz) whole
  kernel corn,
  drained
2 cups milk
3 eggs, beaten
1 small onion, grated
1 teaspoon sugar
1 tablespoon butter,
  melted
Salt and pepper

Mix the ingredients and pour into a greased 1½-quart baking dish. Place in a baking pan containing 1 inch of boiling water.

Cook in a 350° oven for about 45 minutes or until a knife inserted into the center comes out clean. If desired, garnish with parsley.

4 to 6 servings

Zucchini Casserole

2 lb zucchini
Salt and pepper
1 teaspoon dried
  oregano
1 cup shredded Brick
  cheese
½ cup chopped
  almonds
2 tablespoons butter

Steam the zucchini until just tender. Cut into ½-inch slices and layer one-quarter of these in a greased 1½-quart casserole. Sprinkle with salt and pepper and one-quarter of the oregano. Cover with one-quarter of the cheese. Continue making layers in this way, ending with cheese.

Scatter the nuts over the top and dot with the butter. Bake in a 350° oven for 20 minutes.

4 to 6 servings

Spinach and Bacon Bake

1½ lb spinach
4 slices bacon, diced
1 cup sliced
   mushrooms
Salt and pepper
½ teaspoon dried
   thyme
1¼ cups sour cream
¼ cup shredded
   sharp Cheddar
   cheese
¼ cup grated
   Parmesan cheese

Cook the spinach, with only the water clinging to the leaves after washing, until just wilted. Drain well, squeezing out all the excess moisture, then chop. Spread the chopped spinach over the bottom of a greased 1½-quart baking dish. Sauté the bacon in a skillet until crisp. Drain on paper towels and scatter over the spinach. Cover with the mushrooms, then season with salt and pepper and sprinkle with thyme. Bake in a 325° oven for 15 minutes.

Spoon the sour cream over the spinach. Mix together the Cheddar and Parmesan cheeses and scatter over the top. Return to the oven and bake 10 minutes longer, or until the cheese has melted.

4 to 6 servings

RICE, BEANS & PASTA

Macaroni and Cheese with Sour Cream

8 oz elbow macaroni
Salt and pepper
2 tablespoons butter, melted
1½ cups shredded sharp Cheddar cheese
⅔ cup sour cream
¼ cup milk
1 egg, beaten
Pinch of paprika

Cook the macaroni in boiling salted water until just tender. Drain, then mix with the butter; add salt and pepper. Make alternate layers of macaroni and cheese in a greased 1½-quart casserole, reserving about 2 tablespoons of the cheese for the topping.

Mix together the sour cream, milk and egg; add paprika, salt and pepper. Pour over the macaroni and scatter the remaining cheese on top. Bake in a 400° oven for about 20 minutes, or until the top is golden brown. Serve with a green salad.

4 servings

Macaroni and Cheese with Sour Cream; Lasagne (page 82); Fettuccine Casserole

Fettuccine Casserole

8 oz spinach noodles
½ lb sweet Italian
  sausage, casings
  removed, chopped
1 onion, chopped
1 clove garlic,
  chopped (optional)
1 cup sliced
  mushrooms
½ lb ricotta cheese
1 egg
1 teaspoon mixed
  Italian seasoning
  (optional)
1 cup grated
  mozzarella or
  Gruyère cheese

Cook the noodles in boiling salted water until just tender.

Meanwhile, cook the sausage in a 10-inch skillet until browned. Remove the sausage from the skillet and pour off the excess fat; add the onion and garlic and sauté until softened. Add the mushrooms and sauté 3 minutes longer. Stir in the sausage.

Drain the noodles; fold into sausage mixture. Beat the ricotta cheese and egg together; stir into the noodle mixture with the herbs, salt and pepper. Spoon into a greased 2-quart baking dish and top with the mozzarella. Bake in a 350° oven for 25 minutes.

4 servings

Lasagne

2 tablespoons olive oil
2 onions, chopped
1 clove garlic, chopped
½ lb lean ground beef
2 cans (16 oz each) whole tomatoes
¼ cup tomato paste
¾ cup water
1½ teaspoons sugar
2 teaspoons Italian seasoning
1 bay leaf
½ lb mushrooms, sliced
Salt and pepper
8 oz lasagne noodles
1 lb ricotta cheese
1 lb mozzarella cheese, sliced
½ cup grated Parmesan cheese

Heat the oil in a 10-inch skillet, add the onions and garlic, and sauté until softened. Add the beef and sauté until browned, then stir in the tomatoes with their juice, tomato paste, water, sugar and herbs. Bring to a boil and simmer gently for 1¼ hours. Stir in the mushrooms and simmer 20 minutes longer. Discard the bay leaf. Add salt and pepper to taste.

Just before the sauce is ready, cook the lasagne in boiling salted water. (A little oil added to the water will prevent the pasta from sticking together.) Drain.

Spoon a little of the sauce onto the bottom of a 3-quart baking dish. Cover with a layer of lasagne, then a layer each of ricotta, mozzarella and Parmesan cheese, then a layer of sauce. Continue making layers in this way, ending with lasagne sprinkled with Parmesan. Bake in a 350° oven for 1 hour. Serve with a salad.

6 to 8 servings

Illustrated on page 81

Noodles Paprika

8 oz egg noodles
Salt and pepper
1 tablespoon butter
1 onion, finely chopped
1 clove garlic, chopped
2 teaspoons paprika
½ lb cottage cheese
1 cup sour cream
Few drops of hot pepper sauce
1 teaspoon caraway seeds (optional)

Cook the noodles in boiling salted water until just tender. Drain. Melt the butter in a 10-inch skillet, add the onion and garlic and sauté until softened. Stir in the paprika. Cook, stirring, for 1 minute.

Remove from the heat and stir in the cottage cheese, sour cream, hot pepper sauce and caraway seeds. Fold in the noodles. Add salt and pepper.

Spoon into a greased 1½-quart baking dish and bake in a 350° oven for 30 minutes. Sprinkle with paprika. Delicious served with cold sliced meat.

4 servings

Cheese Bake

6 tablespoons butter
12 thick slices bread
1 cup shredded sharp
   Cheddar cheese
1½ cups milk
2 eggs, beaten
Pinch of dry mustard
2 tablespoons
   chopped chives
Salt and pepper

Butter the bread slices. Cut 4 or 5 slices into 1-inch-wide fingers and use to line a 2-quart soufflé mold, buttered sides against the mold. Cut the remaining slices into cubes. Make alternate layers of bread cubes and grated cheese in the mold.

Mix together the milk, eggs, mustard, chives, salt and pepper and pour into the mold. Bake in a 350° oven for 30 minutes. If desired, serve with a tray of raw vegetables.

4 servings

Italian Baked Beans

1 lb dried navy
  beans, soaked
  overnight
¼ lb Italian sausage,
  chopped
2 cloves garlic,
  chopped
2 teaspoons dried
  oregano
Salt and pepper
¼ cup tomato paste
2½ cups water

Drain the beans and mix with the sausage, garlic, oregano, salt and pepper. Mix the tomato paste with the water.

Put the bean mixture in a 2-quart casserole and pour in enough liquid to just cover the beans.

Cover and bake in a 275° oven for 3 to 3½ hours, or until the beans are tender. If necessary, add a little more liquid to the casserole during cooking.

6 servings

Boston Baked Beans

1 lb dried navy
  beans, soaked
  overnight
4 cups water
½ cup firmly packed
  brown sugar
1 teaspoon dry
  mustard
6 tablespoons
  molasses
Salt and pepper
¼ lb salt pork, diced
1 onion, chopped

Drain the beans and put in a saucepan with the water. Bring to a boil, then cover and simmer for about 1 hour, or until the beans are tender. Drain, reserving the liquid.

Mix together the sugar, mustard, molasses, salt and pepper. Put the beans, salt pork and onion in a 2-quart casserole and stir in the molasses mixture. Add enough of the reserved cooking liquid to almost cover the beans.

Cover and bake in a 350° oven for 4 hours, stirring occasionally and, if necessary, adding more of the reserved cooking liquid.

6 to 8 servings

Curried Rice

1½ cups long-grain
   rice
3 cups water
1 onion, finely
   chopped
2 stalks celery, sliced
1 can (8 oz) tomato
   sauce
1½ teaspoons salt
1½ teaspoons curry
   powder (or more if
   desired)
¼ cup butter, melted

Put the rice in a 1½-quart casserole and add the water. Stir in the remaining ingredients.

Cover and bake in a 350° oven for 30 minutes, or until the rice is tender and all the liquid has been absorbed. If desired, serve with hard-cooked eggs and cucumbers in yogurt.

6 servings

Layered Lentil Casserole

1 lb lentils, soaked
  overnight
1 bay leaf
4 slices cooked ham,
  cut into strips
1 teaspoon dried
  thyme
Salt and pepper
2 cups diced cooked
  chicken
1¼ cups chicken
  broth
¼ cup grated
  Parmesan cheese
⅓ cup dry bread
  crumbs

Place the lentils in a saucepan with the bay leaf. Add water to cover and bring to a boil. Simmer gently for about 30 minutes, or until tender. Drain, discarding the bay leaf.

Put about one-third of the lentils in a greased 2-quart casserole. Cover with the ham and sprinkle with half the thyme, salt and pepper. Cover with another third of the lentils, then add the chicken. Sprinkle with the rest of the thyme and salt and pepper to taste.

Top with the remaining lentils and pour in the broth. Cover and bake in a 350° oven for about 30 minutes or until heated through.

Mix together the cheese and breadcrumbs and sprinkle over the top. Bake, uncovered, for 15 minutes, or until the topping is golden brown. Accompany with a tossed green salad and follow with a fruit dessert.

4 to 6 servings

Navy Bean and Corn Casserole

1 cup dried navy
  beans, soaked
  overnight
1 can (12 oz) whole
  kernel corn,
  drained
1 can (16 oz) whole
  tomatoes, drained
  and chopped
Salt and pepper
1 tablespoon brown
  sugar
1 tablespoon grated
  onion
½ cup dry bread
  crumbs

Drain the beans and place in a saucepan. Cover with fresh water, bring to a boil and simmer for 1 hour, or until tender.

Drain the beans and mix with the corn, tomatoes, salt, pepper, sugar and onion. Pour into a greased 1½-quart casserole and sprinkle with the bread crumbs. Bake in a 350° oven for 45 minutes.

4 servings

Fruit and Nut Pilaf

¼ cup golden raisins
1 cup dried mixed
  fruit
1 tablespoon sherry
6 tablespoons butter
1 onion, finely
  chopped
2 cups cooked
  long-grain rice
½ teaspoon ground
  allspice
Salt and pepper
⅓ cup sliced
  almonds, toasted

Put the raisins and dried fruit in a bowl, sprinkle with the sherry and cover with water. Let soak for 4 hours. Drain and chop.

Melt the butter in a skillet, add the onion and sauté until softened. Stir in the rice and allspice, add salt and pepper and mix well.

Fold in the fruit and almonds, then spoon the mixture into a greased 2-quart casserole. Bake in a 375° oven for 30 minutes.

4 to 6 servings

Pearl Barley Casserole

4 tablespoons butter
2 leeks, thinly sliced
1 green pepper, seeded and chopped
1 cup pearl barley
½ cup diced cooked ham (optional)
1 can (12 oz) whole kernel corn, drained
1½ cups chicken broth
Salt and pepper

Melt the butter in a 1½-quart flameproof casserole. Add the leeks and green pepper and sauté until softened. Add the remaining ingredients and stir to combine.

Cover and bake in a 325° oven for 40 minutes, or until the barley is tender and all the liquid is absorbed.

4 servings

Rice with Parsley and Cheese

3 cups cooked long-grain rice
6 green onions, thinly sliced
½ cup chopped parsley
3 eggs, beaten
¼ cup milk
1 cup shredded Cheddar cheese
Salt and pepper

Mix together the rice, green onions and parsley. Combine the remaining ingredients and add to the rice mixture. Mix well, then spoon into a greased baking dish.

Bake in a 350° oven for 30 minutes, or until just set. If desired, serve with sliced tomatoes or a green salad.

4 servings

Spanish Rice Casserole

5 tablespoons olive oil

1 onion, finely chopped

1 clove garlic, chopped

1¼ cups long-grain rice

1 tablespoon chili powder (or more if desired)

¼ lb chorizo or garlic sausage, diced

½ lb mushrooms, sliced

Salt and pepper

2½ cups boiling beef broth

Heat the oil in a 2-quart flameproof casserole, add the onion and garlic and sauté until softened. Stir in the rice and chili powder. Cook, stirring, until the rice is golden. Add the chorizo, mushrooms, salt and pepper; mix well. Add the broth and stir.

Cover tightly and bake in a 350° oven for 30 minutes, or until the rice is tender and the liquid absorbed.

4 servings

INDEX